WHAT IS A
FISH?

Robert Snedden

Photographs by Oxford Scientific Films
Illustrated by Adrian Lascom

Sierra Club Books for Children
San Francisco

For Christopher

The Sierra Club, founded in 1892 by John Muir, has devoted itself to the study and protection of the earth's scenic and ecological resources—mountains, wetlands, woodlands, wild shores and rivers, deserts and plains. The publishing program of the Sierra Club offers books to the public as a nonprofit educational service in the hope that they may enlarge the public's understanding of the Club's basic concerns. The Sierra Club has some sixty chapters in the United States and in Canada. For information about how you may participate in its programs to preserve wilderness and the quality of life, please address inquiries to Sierra Club, 730 Polk Street, San Francisco, CA 94109.

First U.S. Edition 1993

First published in Great Britain in 1993 by Belitha Press Limited, 31 Newington Green, London N16 9PU

Library of Congress Cataloging-in-Publication Data
Snedden, Robert.
 What is a fish?/Robert Snedden; photographs by Oxford Scientific Films; illustrated by Adrian Lascom.
  p. cm.
 Includes index.
 Summary: Describes different types of fish, their breathing, movement, senses, food, defenses, and birth.
 ISBN 0-87156-545-5
 1. Fishes—Juvenile literature. [1. Fishes.]
I. Lascom, Adrian, ill. II. Oxford Scientific Films.
III. Title.
QL617.2.S64 1993
597—dc20   93-6495

Printed in Hong Kong for Imago
10 9 8 7 6 5 4 3 2 1

Editor: Rachel Cooke
Designer: Frances McKay
Consultant: Dr. Jim Flegg
Educational consultant: Brenda Hart

The publisher wishes to thank the following for permission to reproduce copyrighted material:

Oxford Scientific Films and individual copyright holders on the following pages: Fred Bavendam, 6; Fredrik Ehrenstrom, 24 top; Max Gibbs, cover, title page, contents page, 4, 5 bottom, 12 bottom, 17; Laurence Gould, 16; Howard Hall, 8 bottom; Pam and Willy Kemp, 18/19; Breck P. Kent/Animals Animals, 10/11, 27 top; Rudie Kuiter, 5 top, 13 bottom, 20 inset, 26; Zig Leszczynski/Animals Animals, 7 center and bottom, 14, 24 center and bottom; Colin Milkins, 9 bottom; Tsuneo Nakamura, 25 top; J. E. Paling, 7 top; Peter Parks, 13 center, 27 bottom; Robert Redden/Animals Animals, 8 top right; Kathy Tyrrell, 20/21; P. and W. Ward, 25 bottom; W. Wisniewski/Okapia, 11 top; Norbert Wu, 15.

Front cover picture:
A coral trout.

Title page: Clown loaches, such as this one, are found in the rivers of Indonesia.

Contents page: The purple surgeonfish lives in the Red Sea.

CONTENTS

WHAT IS A FISH?

▶ The warty frogfish is found in tropical seas.

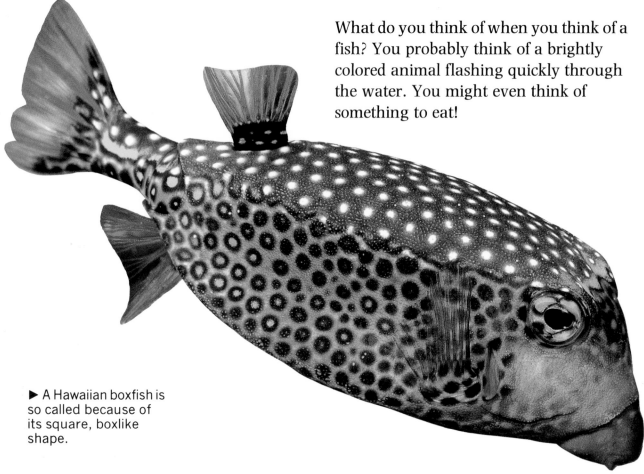

What do you think of when you think of a fish? You probably think of a brightly colored animal flashing quickly through the water. You might even think of something to eat!

▶ A Hawaiian boxfish is so called because of its square, boxlike shape.

▼ The Red Indian fish is found off the coast of Australia.

Fish come in a huge variety of shapes, sizes and colors. They range from the extraordinary Red Indian fish to the jigsaw triggerfish; from the Hawaiian boxfish darting through the coral to the bright red warty frogfish gliding through the ocean.

Yet all fish have certain things in common. These things make them different from the other animals that live in the oceans, lakes and rivers of the world. We shall be looking at some of them in this book.

▼ The jigsaw triggerfish lives on the Great Barrier Reef off the Australian coast.

TYPES OF FISH

There are three main types of fish. First there are the **jawless fish**. These include lampreys and hagfish. They have smooth, slimy skin. They can't swim very well and move by thrashing around. Their mouths tend to be like suckers with lots of small teeth. They feed by attaching themselves to other fish and rasping away their flesh with their teeth.

The second main group of fish are the sharks and rays. Their skin is covered with rough scales. If you stroked a shark it would feel like sandpaper. Most sharks and rays are excellent swimmers that live by catching and eating other animals. They do not have **skeletons** made of bone inside their bodies. Instead, their skeletons are made of a gristle-like tissue called **cartilage**, as are the skeletons of the jawless fish. Cartilage is tough and flexible.

▼ The spotted wobbegong shark is part of the group of fish whose skeletons are made of cartilage rather than bone.

◀ A river lamprey, a type of jawless fish, feeding on a trout, which is a bony fish.

▼ A sea lamprey, showing its sucker mouth.

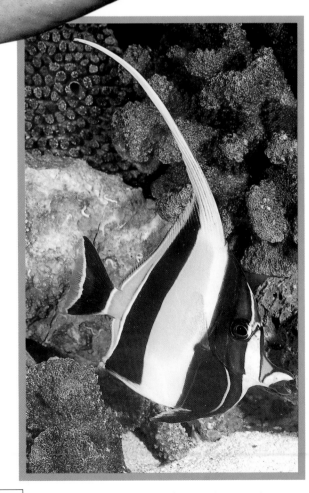

The biggest group of fish are the **bony fish**. As you would guess from the name, their skeletons are made of bone like those of reptiles, birds and mammals. Their skin is covered by smooth scales. There are four times as many different types of bony fish as there are other types of fish. We will look at some other differences between bony fish and other fish later.

Whichever group of fish they belong to, all fish have certain things in common. They all have **gills** to allow them to breathe in water, and they all have **fins** that help them to swim in the water.

A Moorish idol, a colorful bony fish. ▶

BREATHING UNDERWATER

In order to live, all animals must have a gas called **oxygen**. Animals that live on land can breathe in oxygen from the air around them. How do fish, which live underwater, manage to get oxygen?

Fish use the oxygen that is dissolved in the water. To get this oxygen fish have to move the water over their gills. Every fish has gills on both sides of its head. Gills do the same job as your **lungs**.

▶ An African lungfish gets most of the oxygen it needs by breathing air rather than water.

▼ This reef shark's gill slits can be seen just behind its head.

The fish takes in water through its mouth in the same way as you breathe in air. This water then passes over its gills. The oxygen in the water moves into the blood in the fish's gills. The oxygen you breathe into your lungs moves into your blood in the same way. The water is then pumped back out from the gills. Bony fish have flaps to protect their gills, and these open to let the water out. Sharks and rays don't have gill flaps. They have gill slits that open as the water flows through.

There are actually fish that can breathe in oxygen from the air. These are called lungfish. They have gills, just like any other fish, but they also have lungs, just like land-living animals. They live in lakes and marshes in Africa, Australia and South America. Sometimes their homes dry up in summer, but the lungfish can survive by burying themselves in the mud and breathing air. When the rain comes again, the lakes fill up and the lungfish can use their gills in the water once more.

Whales and dolphins are not fish, even though they live in the sea all the time. They don't have gills but lungs. They can stay underwater for a very long time but must come to the surface eventually to breathe air. Whales and dolphins are, in fact, mammals, as are humans.

Did you know?

Most fish breathe by opening and shutting their mouths gently to get water flowing over their gills. Some sharks, however, just swim along with their mouths open all the time.

▼ The cutaway diagram shows the structure of a bony fish's gills. The gills extract oxygen from the water passing over them, moving it into the fish's blood.

▼ ▼ The photograph *(bottom)* shows how a bony fish's gills are protected by gill flaps.

gills

MOVING UNDERWATER

If you have ever tried swimming underwater, you know that it can be hard work and difficult to go very fast. Yet fish seem to speed through the water, changing direction effortlessly. How do they do it?

The bodies of many fish are shaped to allow them to move smoothly through the water, and some fish can go very quickly indeed. The blue-finned tunny is probably the fastest fish – it can reach nearly forty miles per hour. Almost three-quarters of its weight is powerful body muscle.

If they want to move quickly, fish use the big muscles along their sides. These bend the fish from side to side in a slight S shape. The power to move forward comes from the tail pushing against the water. Many kinds of fish don't move their bodies from side to side, only their tails.

Whales and dolphins don't swim by moving their tails from side to side as fish do. Their tails move up and down.

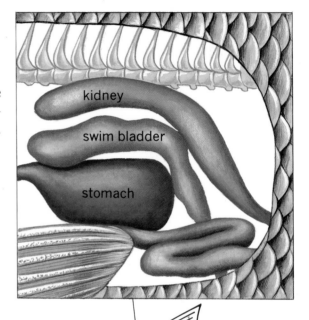

kidney

swim bladder

stomach

▶ The air-filled swim bladder found inside most bony fish allows them to control their depth in the water.

▼ The pickerell's long, thin shape is ideal for fast swimming.

Some fish, such as salmon, can use their powerful body muscles to leap high out of the water, perhaps to escape from danger or to get over something. The fish does this by swimming fast up toward the surface of the water and then giving a strong flick of its tail as it leaves the water.

Most bony fish have an air-filled structure inside them called a **swim bladder**. This lets the fish stay at whatever depth in the water it wants to. If the fish lets more air into its swim bladder, it will rise. If it lets air out, it will sink.

Sharks don't have swim bladders, and people used to think that sharks had to swim all the time to avoid sinking to the bottom of the sea. We now know that a shark's **liver** is particularly large and oily. Oil is lighter than water, so this helps to keep the shark from sinking.

▲ Salmon can use their powerful muscles to leap up waterfalls.

FINS

dorsal fin

pectoral fin

pelvic fin

All fish have fins. A typical fish has several fins, although they can sometimes be hard to see. There is the **dorsal fin** on its back; the **anal fin** on its belly; the **caudal fin** on its tail; a pair of **pectoral fins**, one on either şide, just behind the head; and a pair of **pelvic fins**, usually on the underside, behind the pectorals. Jawless fish don't have pectoral or pelvic fins.

A fish uses its fins to steer with, to balance and to slow down. If it wants to move slowly it will use its fins to row through the water. A few fish, such as sunfish and seahorses, do not have powerful tails and move by using only their fins.

The pectoral fins of the rays look like wings as they seem to flap their way over the sea floor. Flying fish and flying gurnards actually do use their large pectorals to glide through the air.

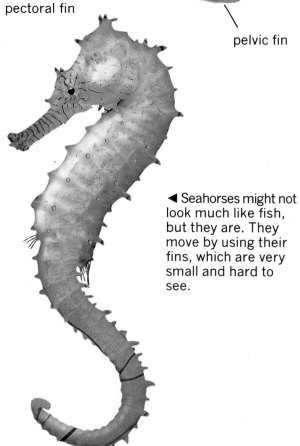

◄ Seahorses might not look much like fish, but they are. They move by using their fins, which are very small and hard to see.

▼ Most fish have fins like those marked on this picture, although they vary enormously in size and shape.

caudal fin

anal fin

Swimming at up to twenty miles per hour, these fish can leave the water altogether and glide on their outstretched pectoral fins. A flight can last for ten seconds before the fish drops back into the sea.

Some fish that live in thick seaweed use their fins like legs to climb through the weed. Tripod fish stand on the bottom of the sea, supported by their pelvic and caudal fins. Mudskippers often come out of the water for a time to look for food on sandy or muddy shores. They move around by walking on their pectoral and pelvic fins.

Flying gurnards leap out of the water and glide through the air for a short distance on their large pectoral fins. ▶

The colorful fins of the lionfish warn other fish of its poisonous spines. ▼

The fins of some fish have an extraordinary shape. Part of the dorsal fin of the deep-sea anglerfish is very stretched out. It is like a fishing line with bait on the end to attract other fish that the anglerfish will eat!

The beautiful waving, brightly colored fins of the lionfish are a warning to others. It has deadly poisonous spines.

SEEING UNDERWATER

The eyes of a fish are similar to the eyes of humans and many other animals. But there are differences. The part of the eye that makes the image sharp is called the **lens**. In humans the lens is oval in shape, but in fish it is almost perfectly round. The part of the eye that controls the amount of light that comes in is the black spot at its center. It is called the **pupil**. Human lenses sit just behind the pupils. A fish's lenses bulge out through its pupils.

Most fish have eyes on the sides of their heads. Because the lenses stick out from its head, a fish can see practically all the way around itself. This is a great help since, in the water, danger – or a meal – could come from any direction, including from above and below.

Fish that live deep down in the ocean, where very little light can reach, have huge eyes. Their eyes are very sensitive

lens

pupil

lens

pupil

Mudskippers spend a lot of the time in very shallow water or mud with their eyes sticking out above the surface. ▼

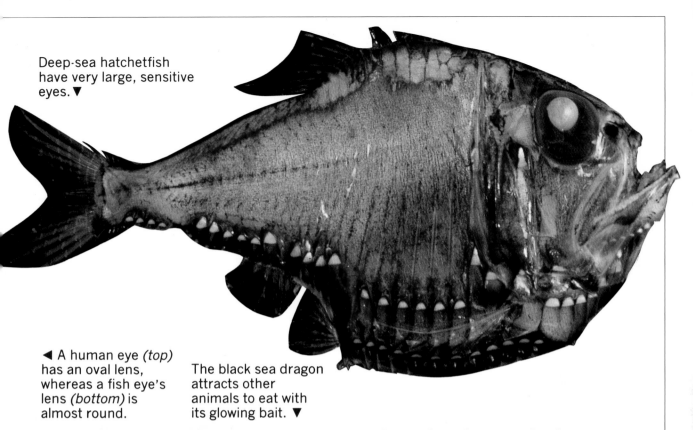

Deep-sea hatchetfish have very large, sensitive eyes. ▼

◄ A human eye *(top)* has an oval lens, whereas a fish eye's lens *(bottom)* is almost round.

The black sea dragon attracts other animals to eat with its glowing bait. ▼

to light. In fact, they may be the most sensitive eyes of any animal.

Some fish live even deeper, where there is no light at all. Their eyes are smaller. They can probably only detect flashes or points of light and not make out shapes. Fish that live at the bottom of the ocean often make their own light to attract other animals that they want to eat. Sea dragons have glowing lures that they use as bait to attract other fish.

One kind of fish appears to have four eyes. In fact, each eye is divided in half. The upper half is suited to seeing in air and the bottom half to seeing in water. These fish swim around near the surface of rivers in Central and South America with the upper halves of their eyes sticking out above the water. This lets them see – and catch – insects skimming over the surface of the river as well as anything edible that might swim by in the water!

HEARING UNDERWATER

At first glance, fish don't appear to have any ears. In fact, for a long time people thought that fish couldn't hear at all. But fish do have ears, and most can hear very well. It's because fish don't have outer ears like you do that they look as if they don't have ears. The flaps on the sides of your head that you call ears are really just the outside parts that help pick up sounds.

Humans have an **eardrum** inside each ear. The sound enters the ear and makes the eardrum vibrate. This vibration is passed on to the part of the ear where the sound is heard.

Fish don't have eardrums. In fact, the ears of most fish don't have openings to the outside at all. A fish's ears are protected inside **capsules** on both sides of its head, just behind its eyes. Sound travels very well through water, better than it does through air. A fish's body, like that of all animals, contains a great deal of water. Sound can travel straight through the fish's body to its ears, where it is heard.

Many types of fish can pick up sounds in another way. Their ears are joined to their swim bladders. The walls of the swim bladder are made to vibrate by the sound traveling through the water, just like an eardrum is vibrated by sound traveling through the air. This vibration is then passed to the fish's ears, usually along a chain of small bones that join them to the swim bladder. Some kinds of fish have tubes (rather than bones) that extend from the swim bladder forward to the ear capsules.

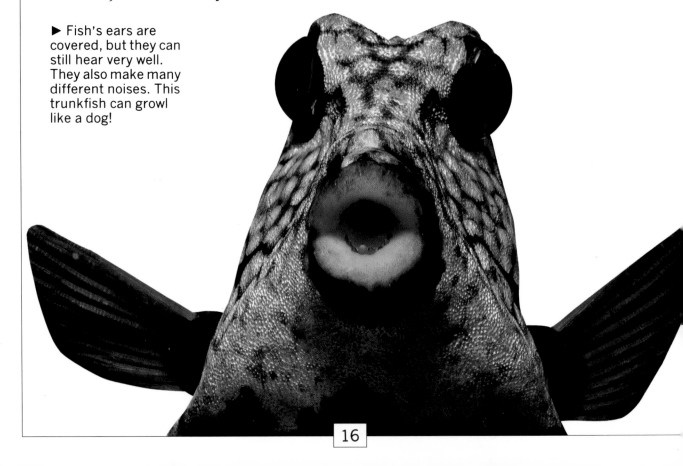

▶ Fish's ears are covered, but they can still hear very well. They also make many different noises. This trunkfish can growl like a dog!

▲ Catfish can make noises by using special drumming muscles that vibrate their swim bladders.

▶ Loaches can make squeaking noises like mice by blowing air from their swim bladders.

Fish often communicate by making noises. Many fish can make powerful calls to one another that can be heard many miles away. Some types of fish make noise by grinding their teeth together, others by rubbing their fins against their bodies. Many fish can use their swim bladders to make sounds as well as to detect them. Special drumming muscles vibrate the swim bladder to make the sounds.

Did you know?

Many fish are very noisy eaters. This means that if one fish finds something to eat, very soon lots of other fish will hear it and come to join in.

A toadfish can be almost as loud as an underground train! It makes a noise to attract female toadfish and to warn off any rival males.

TASTING AND SMELLING

Mammals and birds taste mainly with their tongues, but some kinds of fish can taste with their whole bodies! The parts of you that do the tasting are called **taste buds**, and these are found mostly on your tongue. A fish's taste buds are not only in its mouth but also around its head and pectoral fins and even on its body.

Some fish, such as cod and catfish, have long feelers around their mouths. These are called **barbels**, and they have taste buds, too. The fish uses them to find food hidden in muddy river or lake bottoms.

Fish have nostrils on their heads that they use for smelling just like other large animals. They never use their nostrils to breathe through. Sharks have an incredibly good sense of smell. They can detect the blood of a wounded fish or other animal in the water from a great distance.

Salmon spend the first part of their lives in rivers but as adults live in the ocean. They always return to the river where they were born to lay and **fertilize** their eggs. They find the right river by remembering how it smelled and tasted.

When injured, some fish make a smell to warn other fish. If the skin of a minnow is broken—perhaps when it is bitten by another fish—it produces an alarm substance. Other minnows smell this and swim away from the danger.

◀ The smell of blood often attracts large numbers of sharks. Their excellent sense of smell leads sharks quickly to food.

FISH SENSES

As well as being able to see, smell, taste and hear, fish have special senses of their own. Along each side of their bodies, just under the skin, most fish have a line of sensitive detectors that can pick up the slightest movement of the water around them. These are called **lateral lines**.

Tiny pores or pits in the skin along the lateral lines are open to the water. These let the fish feel any slight difference in **pressure** along its body. It can use this information to tell from which direction a disturbance is coming.

Lateral line detectors on a fish's head can tell the fish if it is about to swim into something by enabling the fish to feel the water pushing against the object. This is why you almost never see a fish swim into the glass wall of a fish tank.

Fish that live in large groups, called **schools** or **shoals**, may use their lateral line sense as well as their sight to avoid

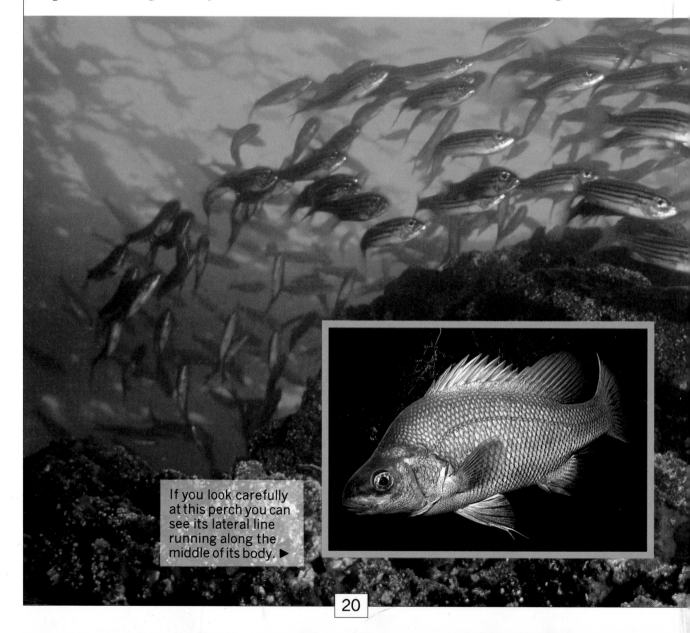

If you look carefully at this perch you can see its lateral line running along the middle of its body. ▶

colliding with one another. Sometimes when a shoal is attacked, the fish flash off in all directions. Each fish could be traveling twenty times its own length in a second. But they never collide!

Some fish can detect tiny **electric currents** in the water. Dogfish can find the fish they eat even when they are buried in the sand at the bottom of the sea. The muscles of all animals produce tiny amounts of electricity when they work.

The dogfish can detect this electricity coming from other fish.

Electric eels and some other fish have special muscles that can produce large amounts of electricity. This electricity is powerful enough to stun other animals. Electric eels can also use their electricity to find their way about in the murky water where they live. They do this by sensing the way the electric current spreads through the water.

Fish such as this school of sardines can swim together in large groups without colliding with one another. ▼

FISH FOOD

▲ The great white shark's teeth are a special kind of scale. They are excellent tools for this active hunter.

▲ Angelfish have strong jaws and teeth to cut through the coral that they eat.

If there is something in the water that can be eaten, then it is almost certain that somewhere there is a fish that can eat it!

There are fish that eat plants and fish that eat other fish; just as on land there are animals that eat plants and animals that eat other animals. Many river fish will eat the plants that grow along the river's edge. There are fish that will eat the simple plants called **algae** that often grow on rocks.

In the ocean many fish live by mainly eating **plankton**. Plankton are tiny plants and animals that float in the water. The biggest fish of all, whale sharks and basking sharks, live on plankton. They have special mouth parts called **gill-rakers**. These strain the tiny plankton out of the water before it passes through their gills. Other fish that feed on plankton also have gill-rakers.

Most fish are **carnivores**. This means that they eat other animals – including other fish! The teeth of some kinds of fish are joined together into sharp-edged

gill-rakers

plates. These are fish that
feed on hard coral or hard-shelled
shellfish, such as oysters and mussels.

Others, such as many sharks and tuna,
are fast, active hunters. Sharks' teeth are
unlike those of other fish. They are, in fact,
a special kind of scale. A shark has several
rows of teeth in its jaw, lying one behind
the other. Usually only the row of teeth at
the front is actually in use. As these teeth
are worn or damaged they are replaced by
the teeth behind them. They provide a
powerful cutting edge.

Sharks have teeth only in their jaws,
but bony fish can have teeth on their
tongues and in their throats, as well as
along their jaws. Many fish have strong,
sharply pointed teeth that they use to
catch their prey.

Some types of fish have jaws that can
open up enormously. In the deepest parts
of the ocean there may not be very much
to eat. This means that it is important to be
able to eat anything that is found. Some
deep-sea fish have jaws and bellies that
can stretch so much they can actually
swallow fish that are bigger than they are!

▲ A basking shark's
gill-rakers strain the
plankton that they eat
from the water.

► River fish such as
these goldfish (a type
of carp) live off the
plants that grow on the
river's bed and banks.

23

FISH DEFENSES

As well as finding enough to eat, fish must try to make sure that they aren't eaten themselves. Many fish do this by hiding themselves. Flatfish, which live on the bottom of the sea, have colored markings that blend in with the seabed. The fish can actually change the shape and color of its **camouflage** markings to suit the background it finds itself against.

Many ocean-swimming fish have dark-colored backs and silvery bellies and sides. This makes them very difficult to see from above, where they blend with the dark ocean, or from below, where they blend with the light from the sky.

Some types of fish camouflage themselves by looking like seaweed. Others look like dead leaves floating on a river. Still other fish look like rocks.

Some fish appear to be dangerous when they are not. One type of eel looks just like a poisonous sea snake. Weever fish, which often lie half buried in the sand, have poisonous spines on their gill

▼ Stonefish *(top)* are difficult to see. They also have poisonous spines.

▼ This Sargassum fish *(center)* looks just like a piece of seaweed.

◄ The anemone fish is protected by the stinging tentacles of the sea anemone.

flaps. They will raise these poisonous spines if they are disturbed. Sole don't have poisonous spines, but they pretend that they do by raising a fin.

Many fish protect themselves by making themselves difficult to eat. Puffer fish and porcupine fish have strong spines on their skin. If they are attacked they make themselves much bigger than normal by swallowing huge amounts of water so that the spines stand out.

There are also fish that are very poisonous. Weever fish have already been mentioned; they are poisonous enough to kill a human. Several other kinds of fish, such as toadfish and stonefish, are just as dangerous.

▲ This spiny puffer fish has made its spines stand out to protect itself.

▼ A leaf-fish is well camouflaged on the seabed.

25

THE NEXT GENERATION

▲ Tiny seahorses emerge from an adult male's pouch.

Most female fish lay eggs, often in very large numbers. In order for young fish to develop inside the eggs, the eggs must be fertilized by a male fish. In a few cases, this takes place before the eggs are laid, but for most fish the eggs are fertilized by the male after they have been laid.

The eggs of many fish simply float freely, unprotected, in the ocean. This means that many of them are eaten by other fish. Some kinds of fish hide their eggs in mud at the bottom of rivers or make a nest for them. A male seahorse gathers up the fertilized eggs and keeps them safe in a pouch on his belly while they grow. Mouthbrooders collect their eggs and carry them around in their mouths until they hatch.

A very few kinds of fish, whose eggs are fertilized inside the female, give birth to live young – for instance, many sharks.

Some fish can actually switch between being male and female. As they grow older they may change from males into females. Others are both male and female at the same time and are able to fertilize their own eggs. Tripod fish, which live on the bottom of the ocean, are like this. Perhaps this is because it is difficult to find a mate in the darkness!

A male anglerfish, another deep-sea fish, is able to find a female by smell. When he does find a female, the small male fish attaches himself to her by his mouth. He remains attached to her for the rest of his life. This means that the female never has to look for a male to fertilize her eggs.

▲ Young rainbow trout hatching from their eggs.

▼ As the female brown trout lays her eggs, the male trout swims beside her to fertilize them.

A WATERY WORLD

Fish have been swimming in the waters of the world since before the time of the dinosaurs. There are fish in nearly all parts of the ocean, from the blackest depths to the sunlit coral reefs. Fish are also found in rivers and lakes. Every year new kinds of fish are discovered.

It is difficult to sum up in a few words what a fish actually is. All fish live in water and breathe through gills. They all have fins to help them move about. Most fish have a lateral line sense, but some other water-living animals do as well.

Only fish have swim bladders, but not all fish do. Most fish lay eggs, but some do not.

The lives of fish and the ways in which they are suited to their watery world are complex and fascinating. So is their vital role in the web of life. Fish depend on other water-living animals and plants for their own survival and in turn provide food for many birds and other animals, including humans. There is still much to understand about fish and their place in our living world.

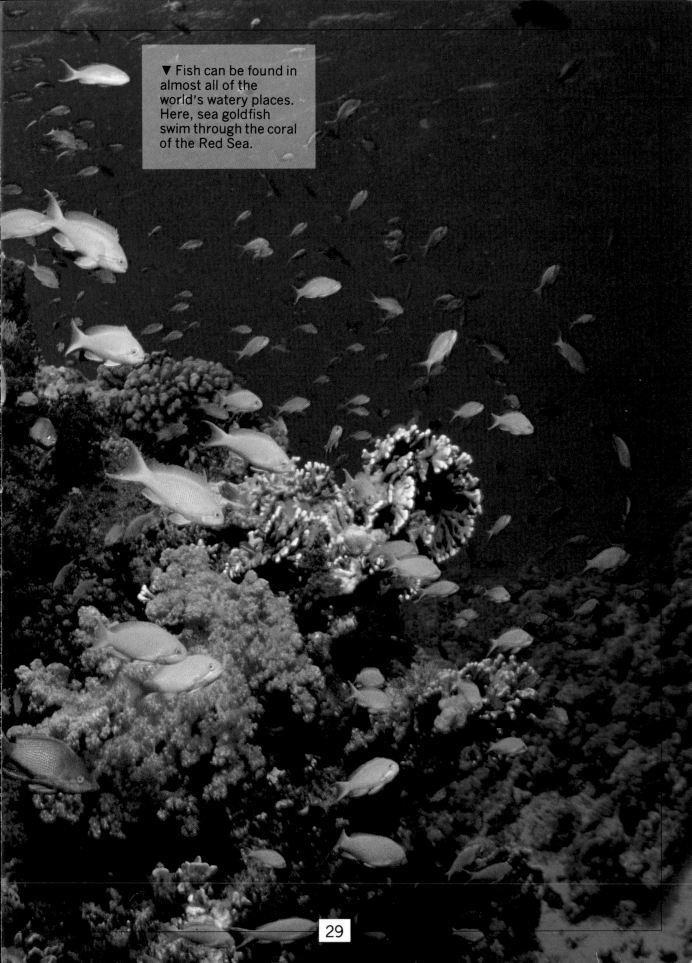

▼ Fish can be found in almost all of the world's watery places. Here, sea goldfish swim through the coral of the Red Sea.

GLOSSARY

Algae: Very simple types of plant often found growing on rocks in wet conditions. Seaweeds are algae.

Barbels: Long feelers around the mouths of certain types of fish. Barbels are used to taste and smell and to find food in places such as muddy river bottoms.

Bony fish: The biggest group of fish. There are more bony fish than there are any other kind. They have *skeletons* made of bone and thin scales covering their bodies.

Camouflage: Colors or patterns on something that help it to blend into its surroundings, making it difficult to see.

Capsule: A small covering that gives protection and support to a part of the body.

Carnivores: Animals that kill and eat other animals.

Cartilage: A tough, flexible tissue that some fish, such as sharks, have instead of bones.

Eardrum: The part of the human ear that is made to vibrate by sound waves. These vibrations are then passed on to the part of the ear where the sound is heard.

Electric current: Electricity is the energy produced by the movement of tiny particles called electrons. Electrons can move through some substances, such as some metals and water, but not others. The flow of electricity through one of these substances is called an electric current.

Fertilize: To join the male sperm with the female egg so that a new animal can grow inside the egg.

Fins: The parts of a fish that help it move in the water.
  Anal fin: The belly fin of a fish, used for balance.
  Caudal fin: The tail fin of a fish, used for fast swimming.
  Dorsal fin: The back fin of a fish, used for balance.
  Pectoral and pelvic fins: The pairs of fins on the side of a fish, used for steering. Jawless fish do not have these pairs of fins.

Gill-rakers: Mouth parts of fish, such as basking sharks, that eat *plankton*. The gill-rakers strain the plankton out of the water the fish swallows before it passes over its *gills.*

Gills: The part of the body that many water-living animals, such as fish and young amphibians, use for breathing.

Jawless fish: One of the three main groups of fish. As their name suggests, they do not have jaws. They have smooth skin, without scales, and do not have *pectoral* or *pelvic fins.*

Lateral line: A line of sensitive detectors found along the sides of most fish and some amphibians that can detect movement and vibrations in water.

Lens: The part of the eye that focuses the light coming into it, creating a sharp image.

Liver: An important part of the body in many animals. It stores food and helps to provide energy for the body. It aids digestion and also gets rid of poisons in the blood.

Lungs: The parts of the body that many types of animal, including humans, use to get *oxygen* from the air.

Oxygen: A gas found in air and dissolved in water. Living things must have oxygen to stay alive.

Plankton: Very tiny plants and animals that float and drift in the seas and oceans.

Pressure: A force pushing on or against something. A body, a liquid or a gas exerts pressure on any other body or surface it touches.

Pupil: The black part in the middle of the eye through which light enters.

School: A large group of fish swimming together, sometimes for protection. Such a group of fish can also be called a shoal.

Shoal: See *School.*

Skeleton: The name given to the bone or cartilage structure inside an animal. The skeleton strengthens the body, protects the soft parts inside and provides somewhere for muscles to be attached.

Swim bladder: The part of the body that fish use to change their depth in the water. They do this by adjusting the amount of air in the swim bladder.

Taste buds: Tiny parts of the body used for tasting. Most land animals have their taste buds mainly on the upper surface of their tongues. Fish can have taste buds all over their bodies.

INDEX